Progress with Oxford

Age 3-4

D1797642

Starting to Write

Hello! I'm Jot.

I'm Dot!

Contents

Key

 Write

 Draw

 Trace with finger

 Trace with pencil

 Play together

 Circle

 Colour

 Match

 Find the sticker

OXFORD
UNIVERSITY PRESS

Busy fingers

 Trace these patterns with your finger.

 **Trace the lines to find out who owns which pencil.**

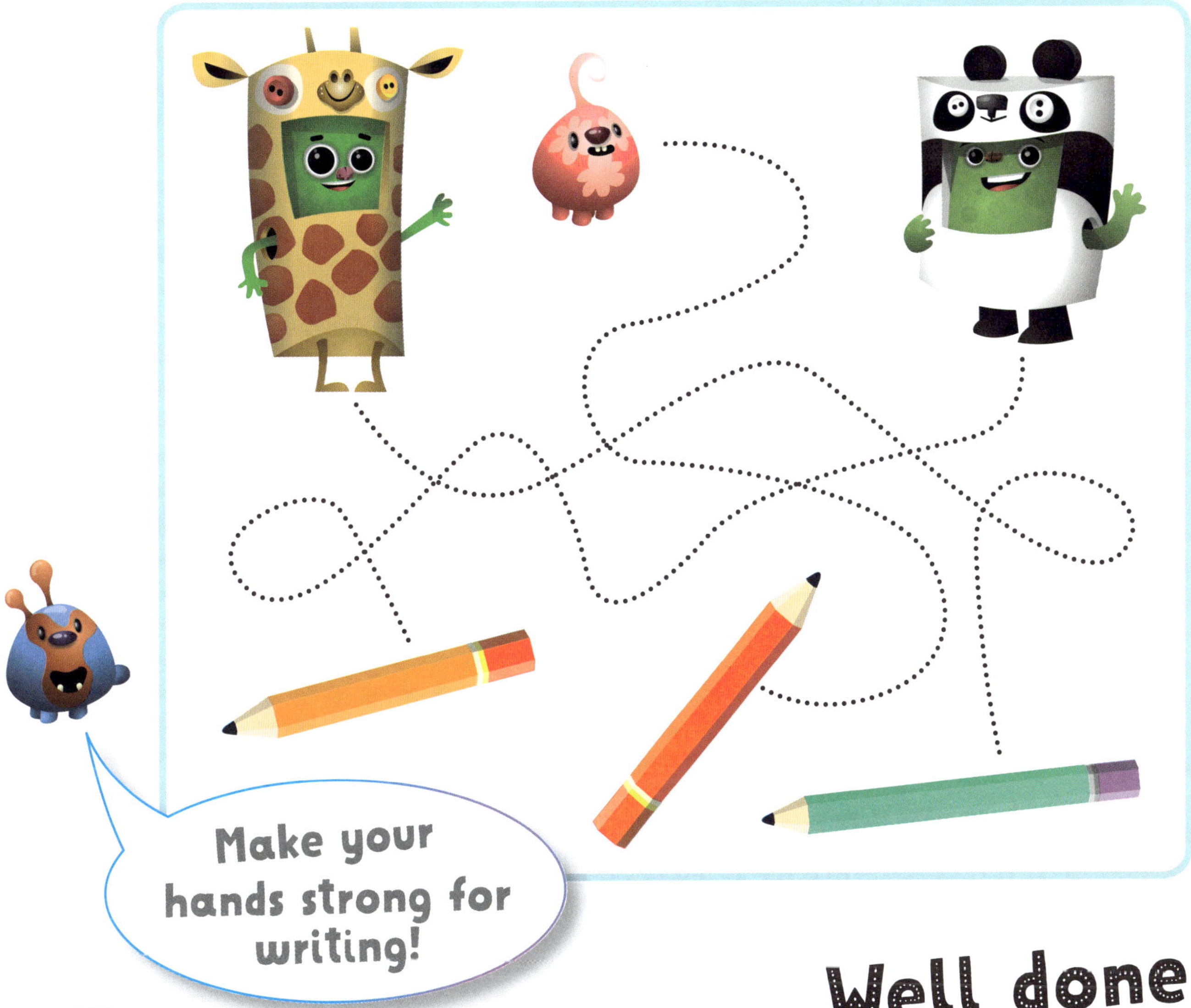

Make your hands strong for writing!

 **Play with writing.**

Use a big brush and water to draw circles and lines on the floor or the wall outdoors.

Hold some play dough in one hand. Squeeze the dough in time to your favourite song. Now try it with the other hand.

Use chalk to draw arrows on a path for a friend to follow.

Well done!

Give yourself a sticker

Pencil time

Pick up your pencil.

Which hand do you hold your pencil in?

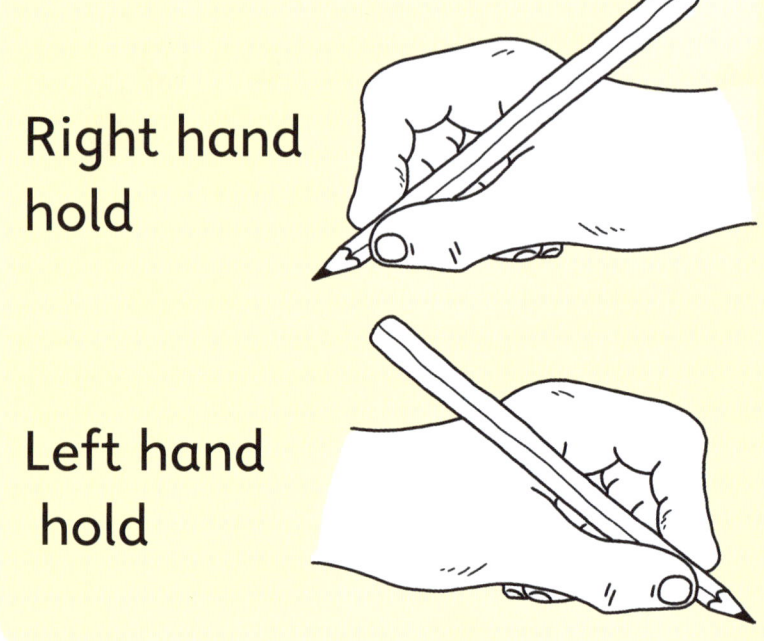

Right hand hold

Left hand hold

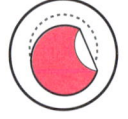 Trace the paths.

Find the sticker with the animal's home.

 Trace these patterns.

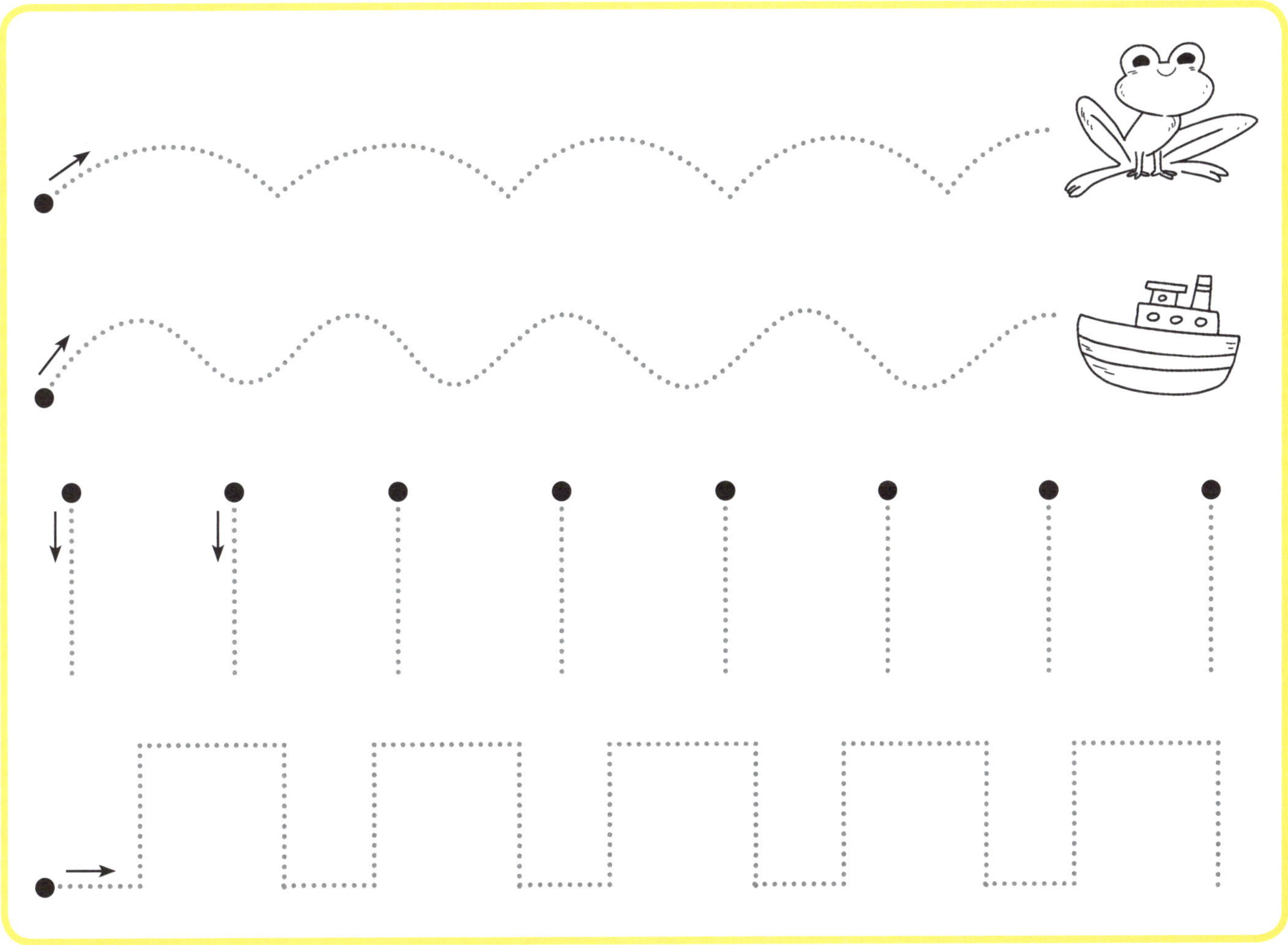

 How many patterns can you make?

 Play with writing.

Try waving pieces of material, ribbons or scarves in the air in different ways to make patterns.

Flatten out some modelling clay and use a stick or a pencil to make patterns in it.

Well done!

Give yourself a sticker

Now – track how you're doing on page 32!

Drawing lines

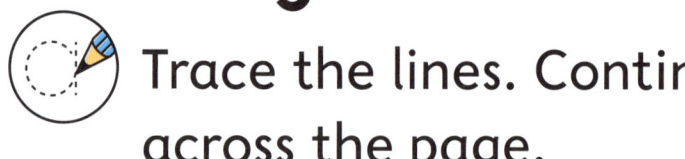 Trace the lines. Continue the pattern across the page.

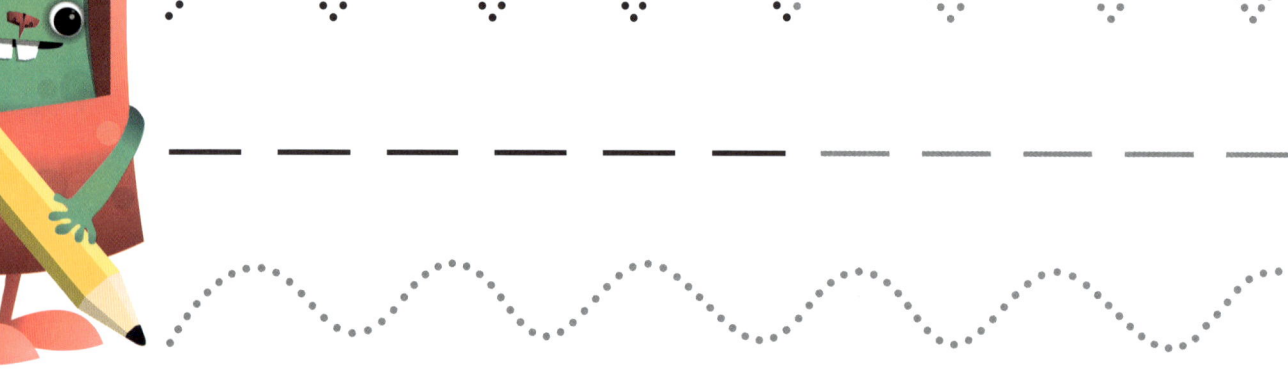

Draw the path to help Dot to his house.

 Draw the line all the way to Jot.

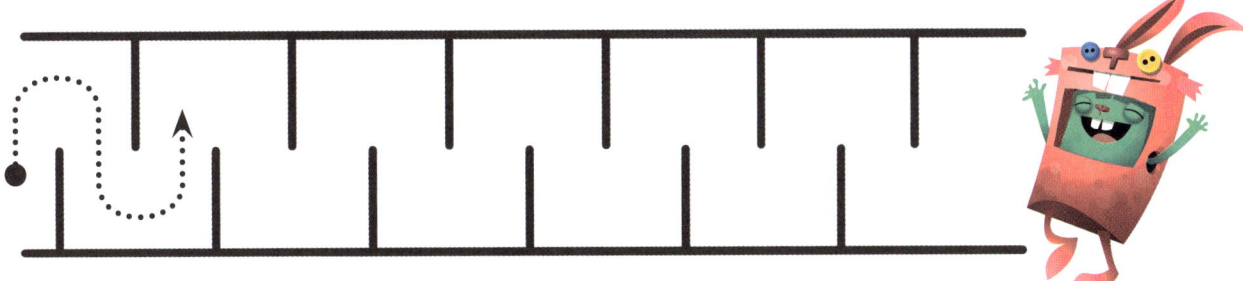

 Draw the path to help Jot find Dot in the maze.

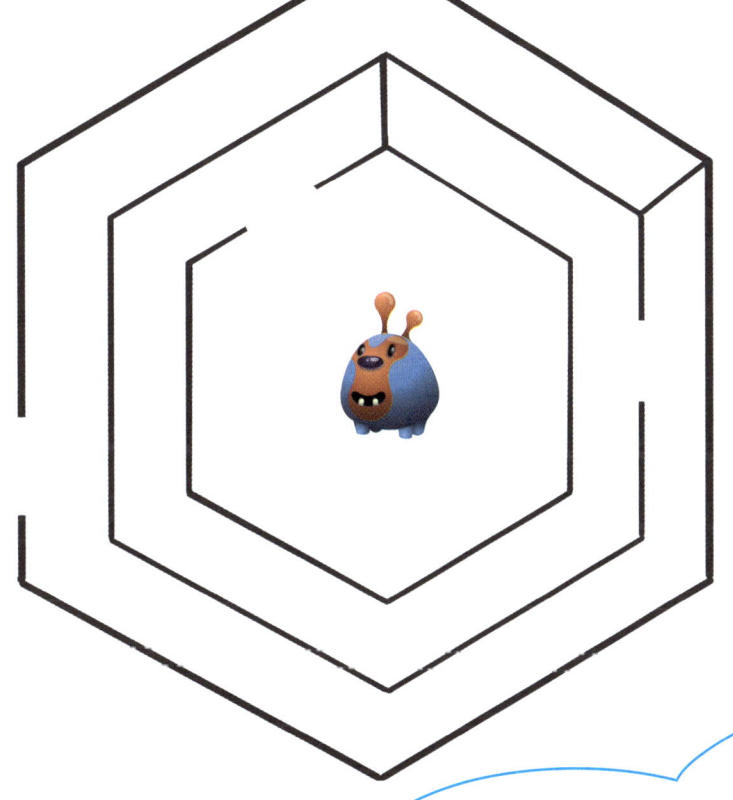

What can you do next?

 Play with writing.

Put some toy bricks on a piece of paper. Draw a path through the bricks.

Create your own mazes outdoors by placing stones or sticks in a line along the path. Then move in and out of them using a paintbrush and water or chalk.

Give yourself a sticker

Now – track how you're doing on page 32!

Getting ready to write

 Trace the curves. Start at the dot each time.

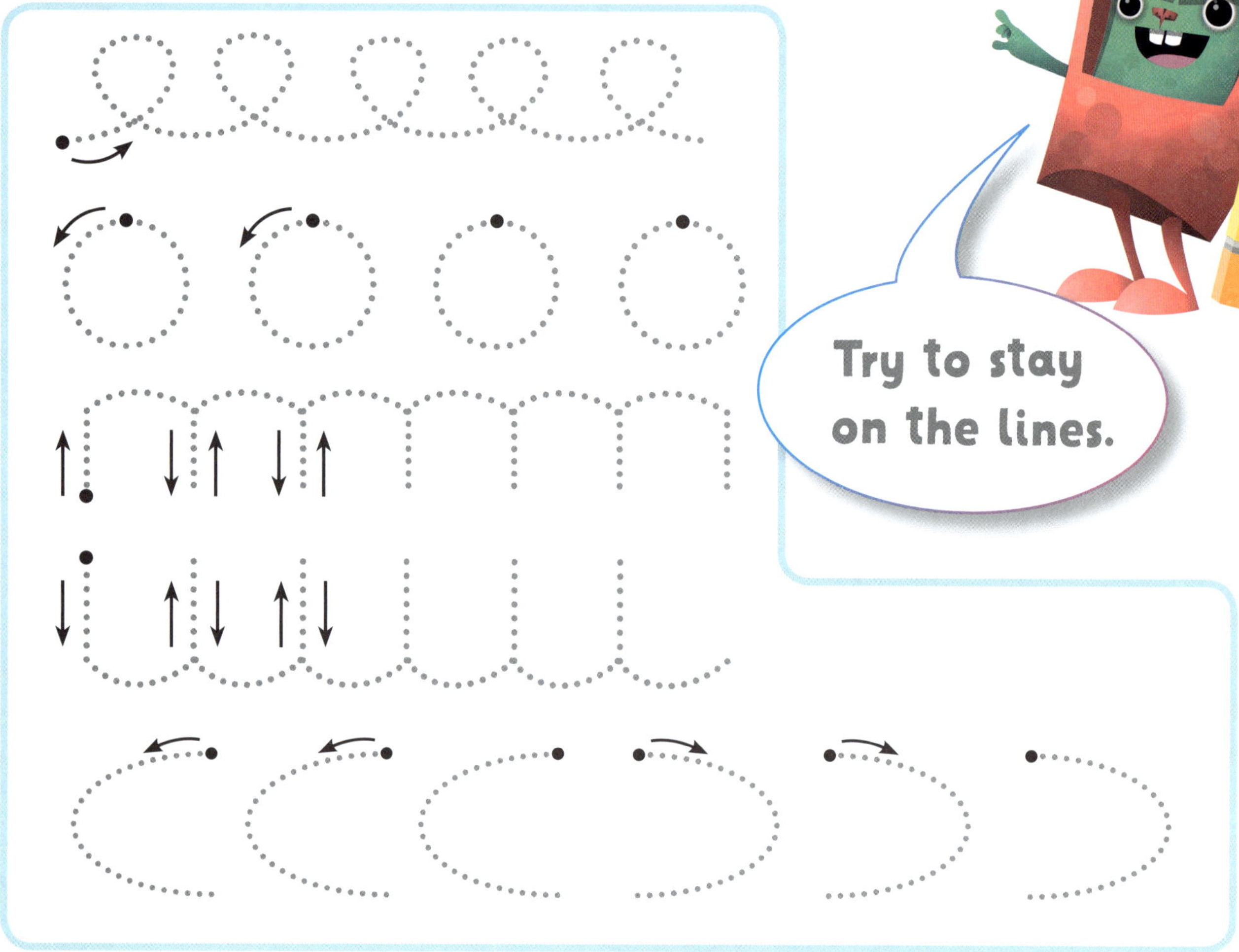

Try to stay on the lines.

 Draw lots of balls for Jot to juggle.

 # Trace these lines.

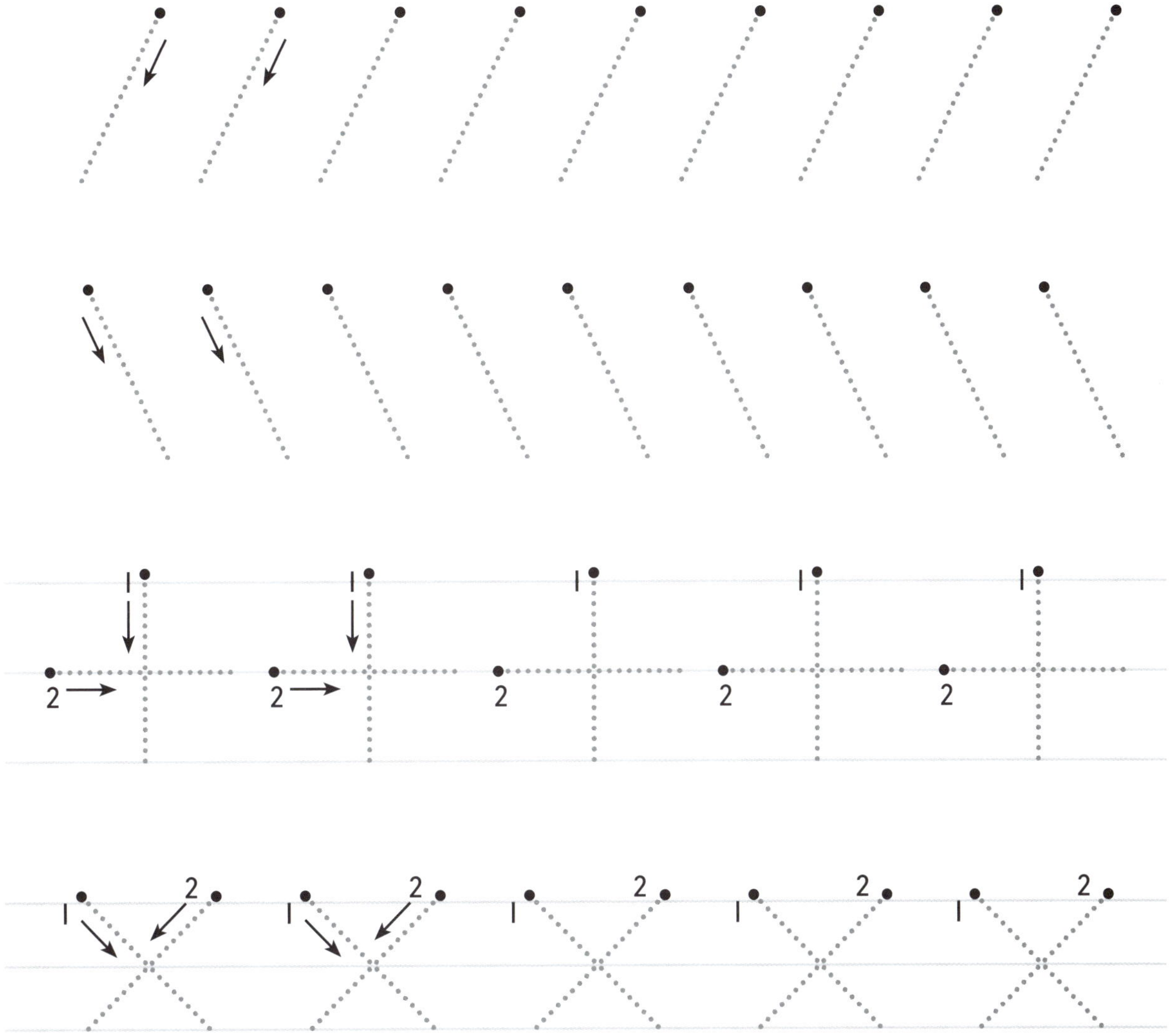

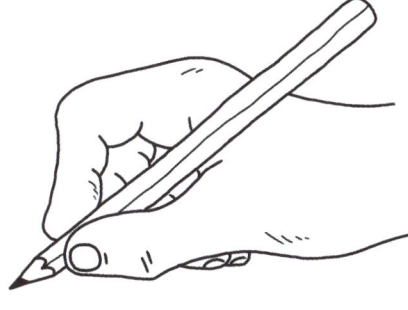

Right hand hold

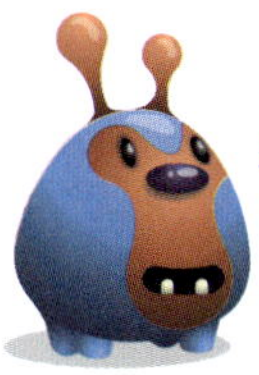

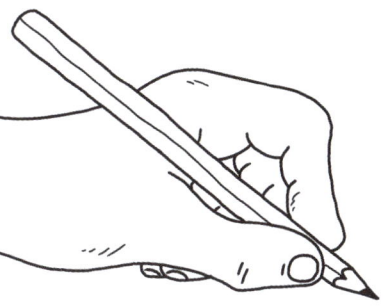

Left hand hold

Give yourself a sticker

Now – track how you're doing on page 32!

Going round (c, a and o)

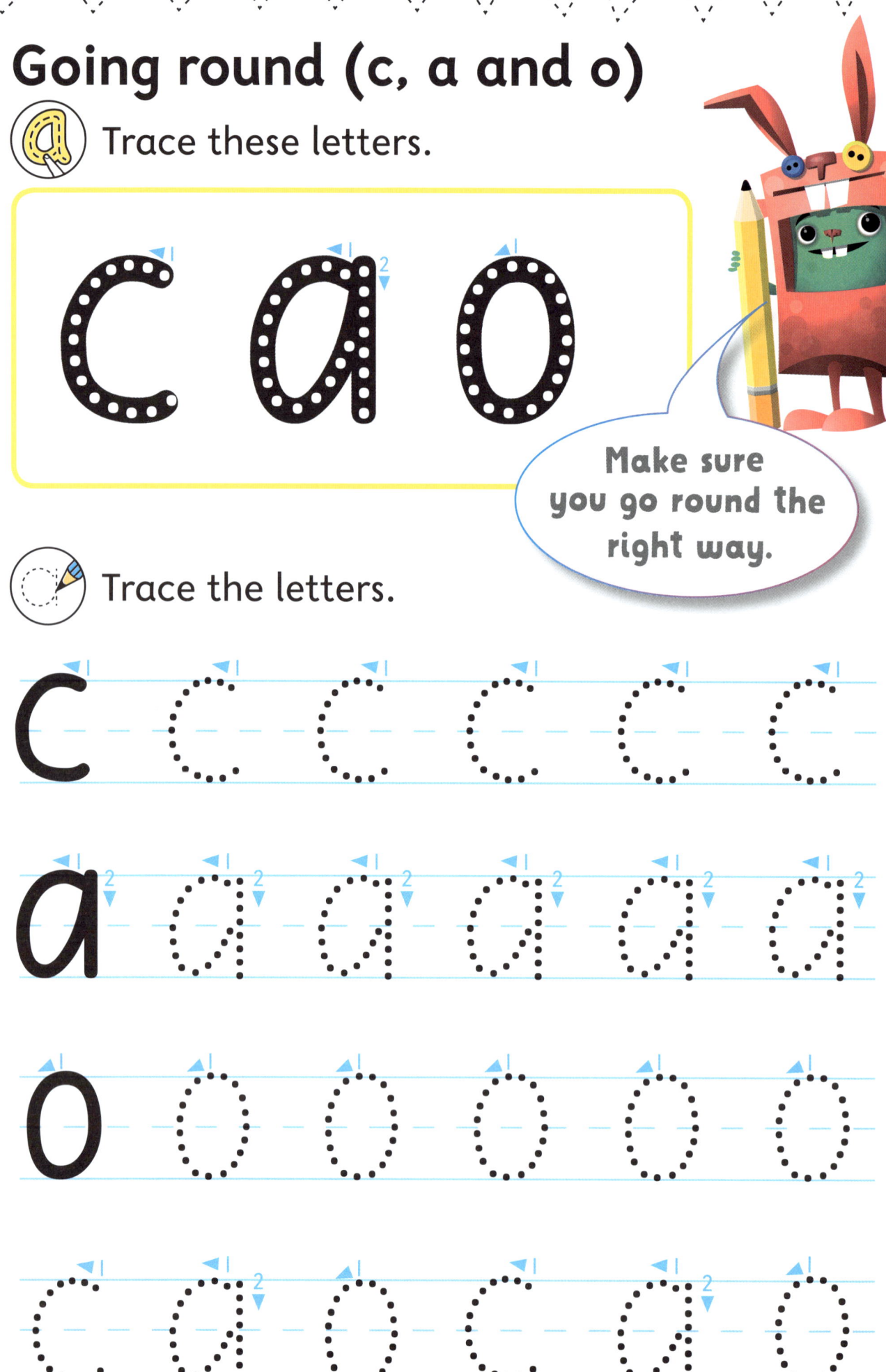

Trace these letters.

c a o

Make sure you go round the right way.

Trace the letters.

c c c c c c

a a a a a a

o o o o o o

c c c c c c

 Colour shapes with **c** in yellow.
Colour shapes with **a** in red.
Colour shapes with **o** in blue.

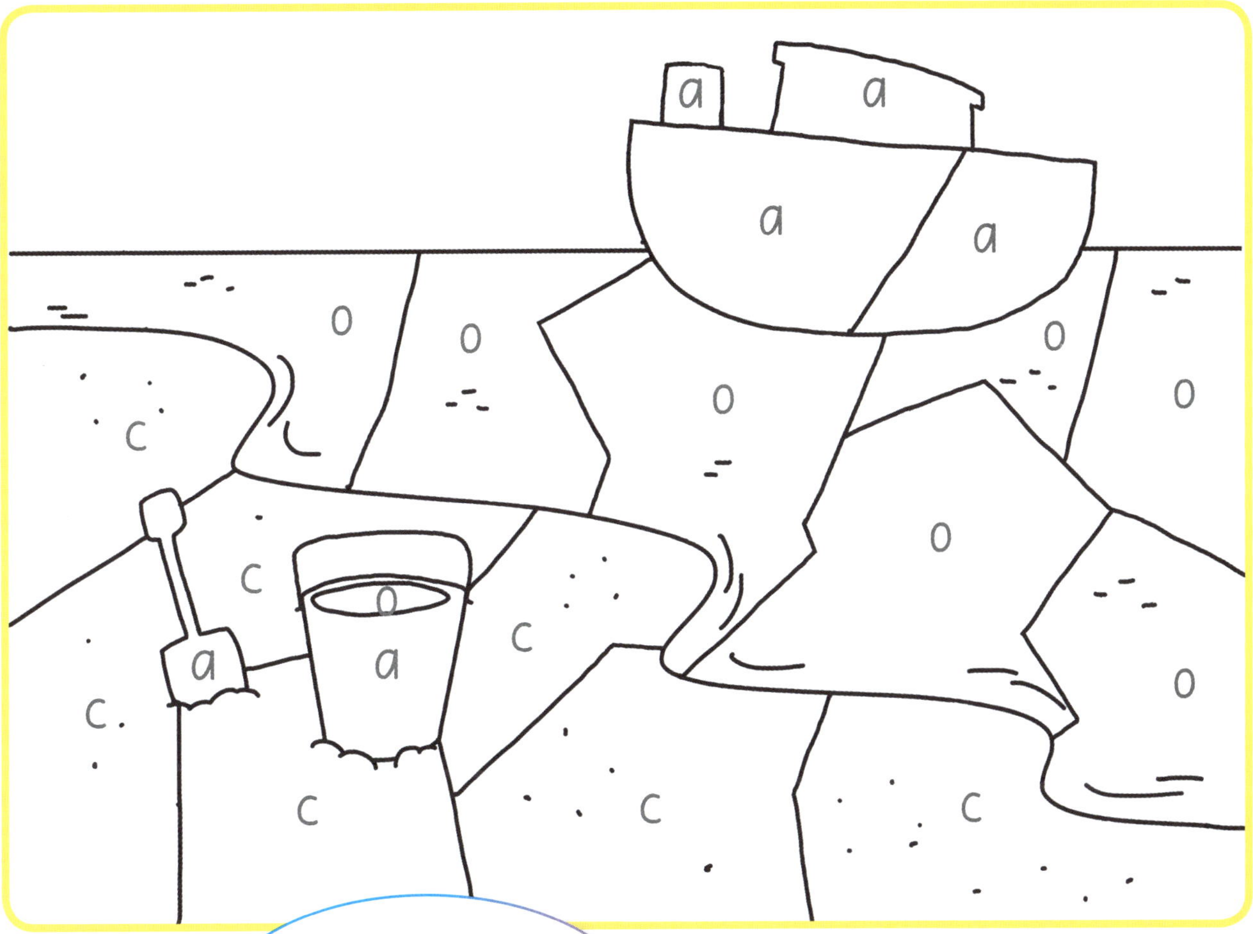

 Can you make up writing games?

Well done!

 Play with writing.

Cover a tray with flour. Write the letters in the flour.

Draw the letters on your friend's back. Can they guess the letter?

Fill a closeable sandwich bag with hair gel and glitter. Close it and flatten it. Write letters in the gel with your finger.

Give yourself a sticker

Now – track how you're doing on page 32!

Round and down (d, g and q)

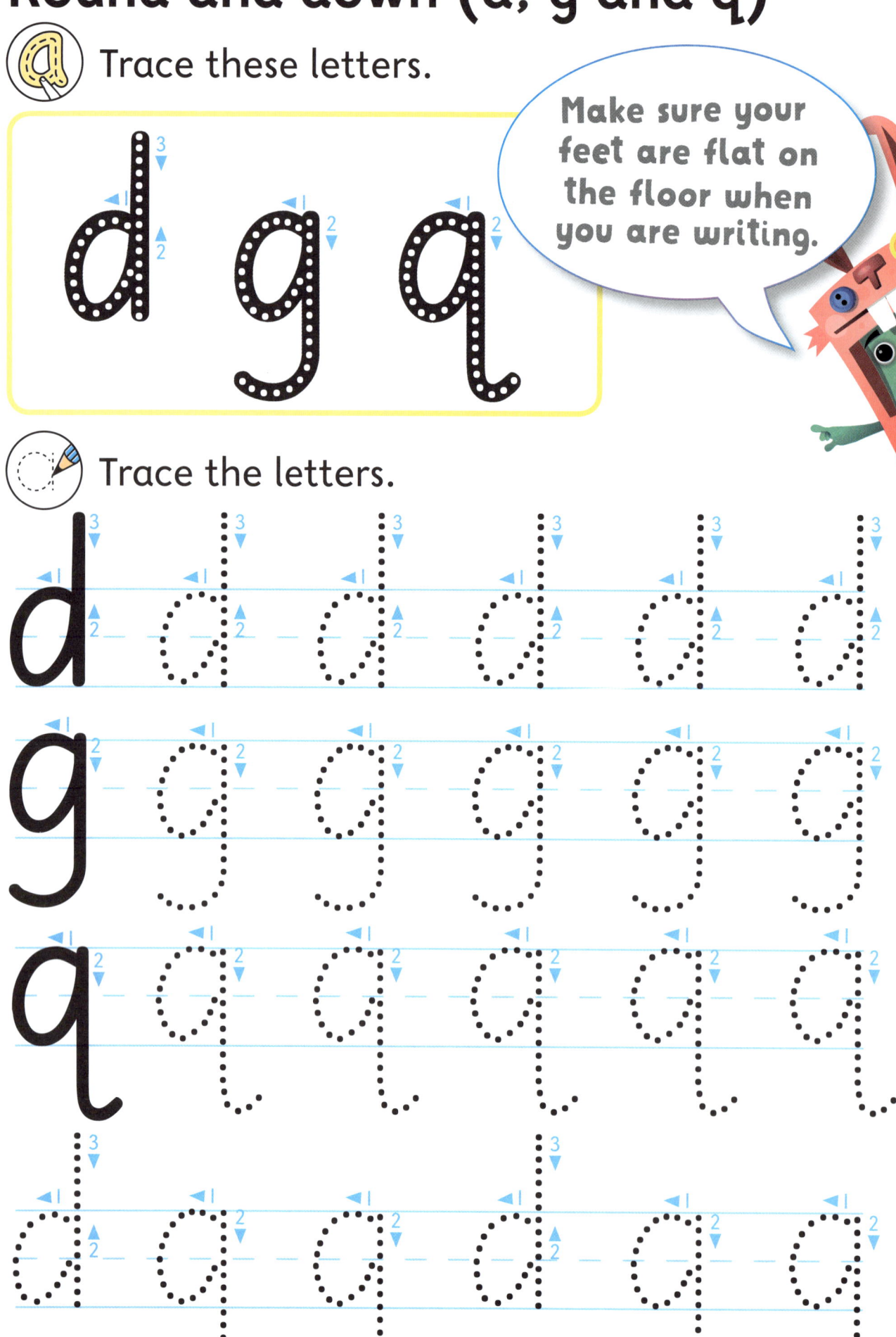

Trace these letters.

d g q

Make sure your feet are flat on the floor when you are writing.

Trace the letters.

 **Join the dots.**

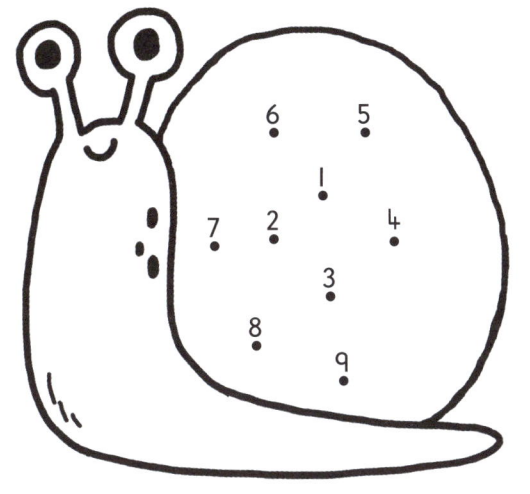

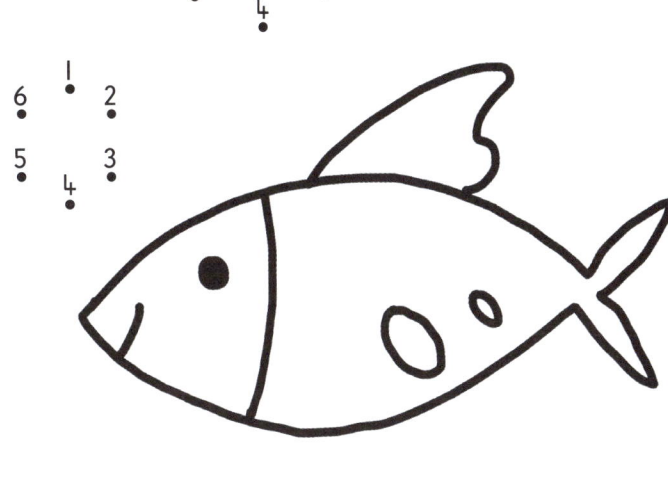

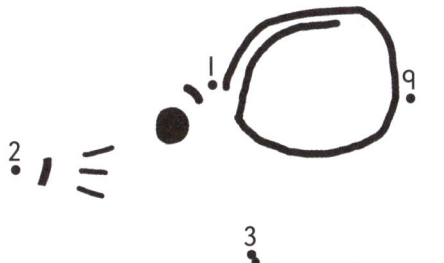

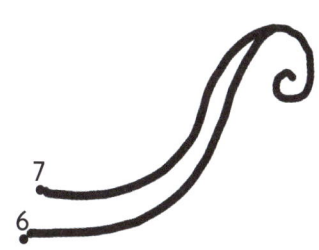

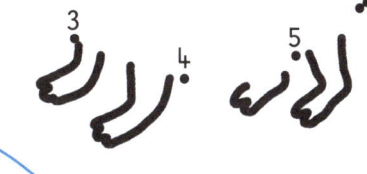

Can you make letter shapes with some modelling clay?

 **Play with writing.**

Tape some kitchen foil to a flat surface. Practise writing **d**, **g** and **q** letter shapes using a paintbrush and your favourite colour paint.

Be a letter detective – can you find letters **d**, **g** and **q** on a walk to the shops?

Well done!

Give yourself a sticker

Now – track how you're doing on page 32!

Round and round (e, f and s)

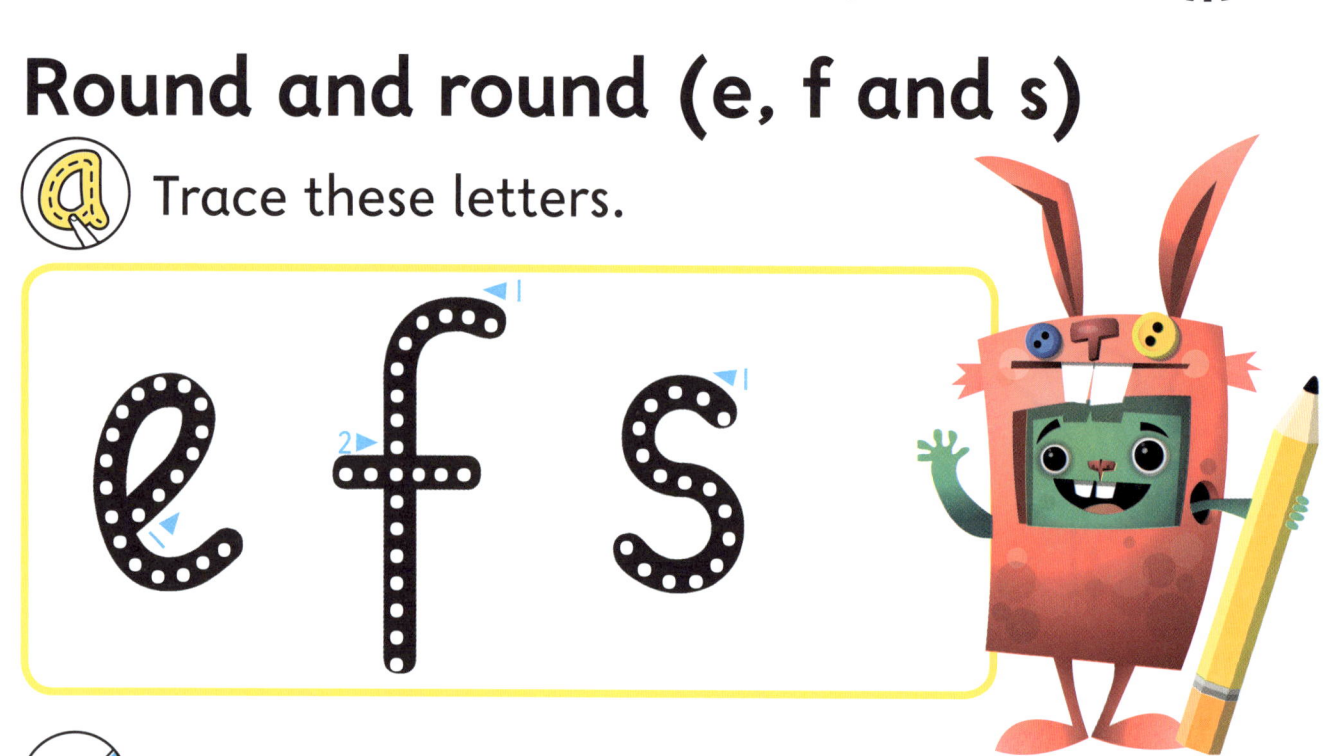

a Trace these letters.

e f s

✎ Trace the letters.

e e e e e e

f f f f f f

s s s s s s

e f s e f s

Trace the letter patterns.

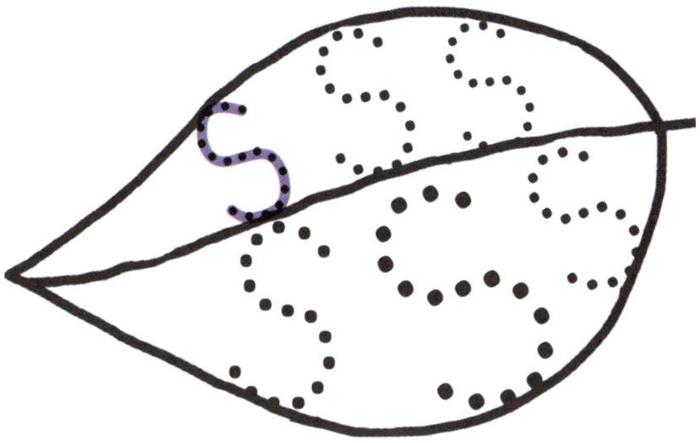

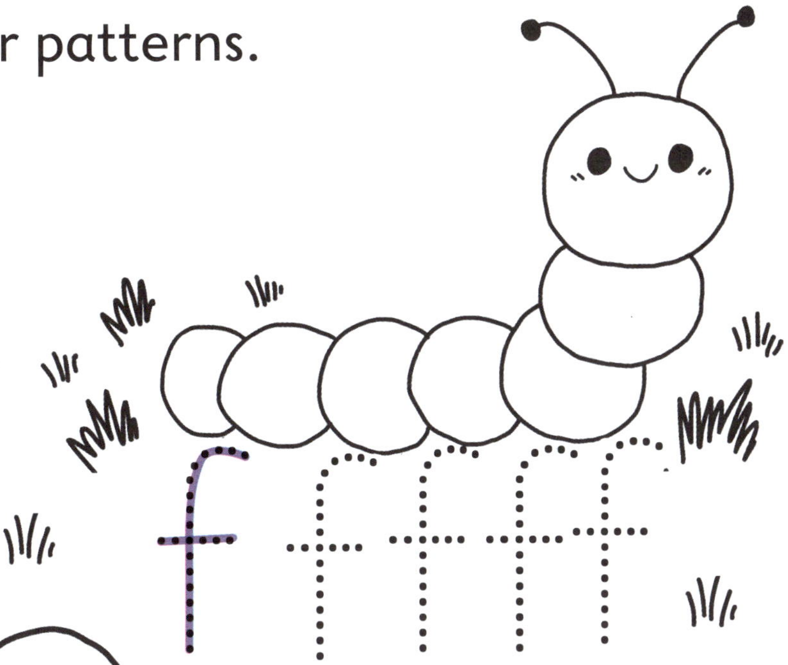

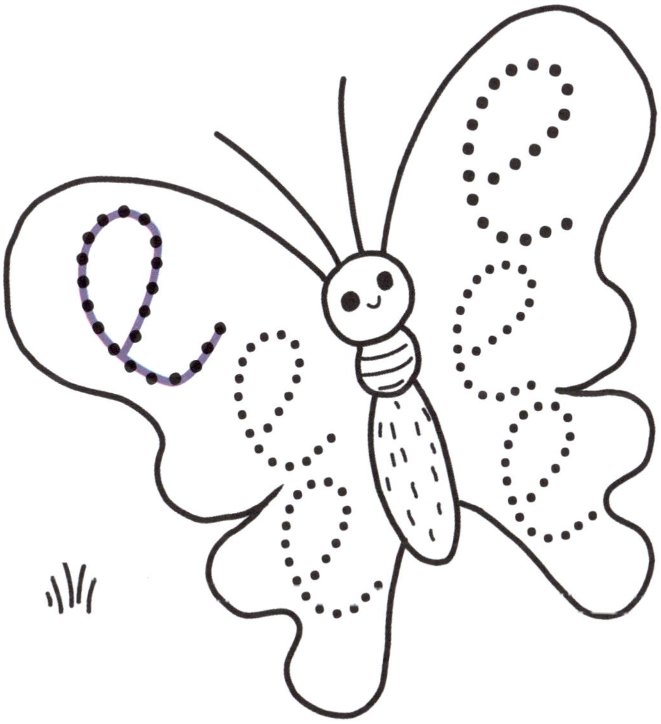

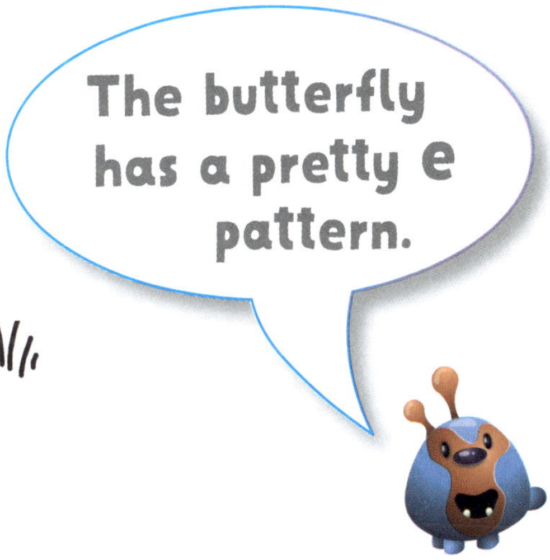

The butterfly has a pretty e pattern.

Well done!

 **Play with writing.**

Draw the letters **e**, **f** and **s** in the air with your finger.

Make a pattern on a path with a rope or some string. Trace around the rope or string with chalk.

Use a stick to draw letters in mud or sand.

Give yourself a sticker

Down, up and over (r and m)

 Trace these letters.

Start at the top, go down to the bottom, then back up again and over.

 Trace the letters.

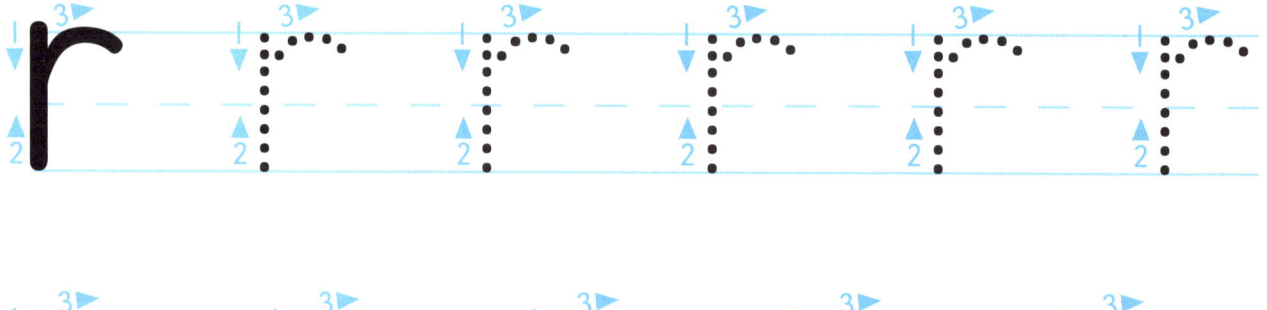

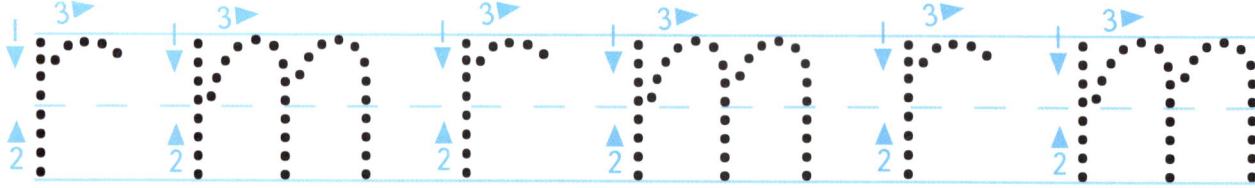

Stickers for page 4

Stickers for page 19

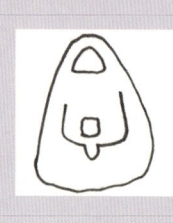      

Stickers for page 25

Character stickers

Reward Stickers

 Trace over the dotted letters in this picture.

 Circle all the letters **r** and **m** in the picture.

Spot the letters in the park!

Give yourself a sticker

Now – track how you're doing on page 32!

More down, up and over (n and h)

(a) Trace these letters.

Start at the top, go down, then back up and over.

(pencil) Trace the letters.

Well done!

Give yourself a sticker

Now – track how you're doing on page 32!

First words

 Trace these letters to make the words.

 Find the stickers of the objects.

can

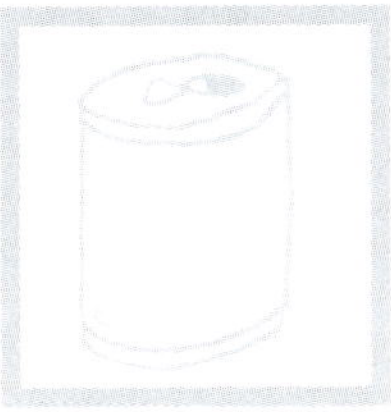

bag

dog

man

hen

fan

horse

egg

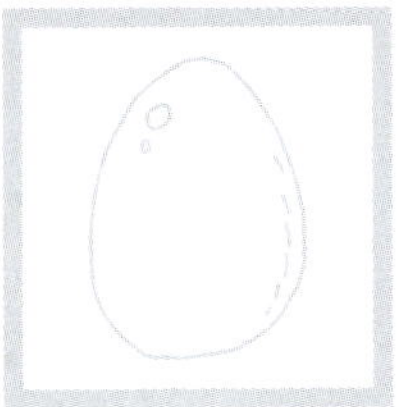

Give yourself a sticker

Now – track how you're doing on page 32!

Straight lines (b, k and l)

 Trace these letters.

These have straight lines going from top to bottom.

 Trace the letters.

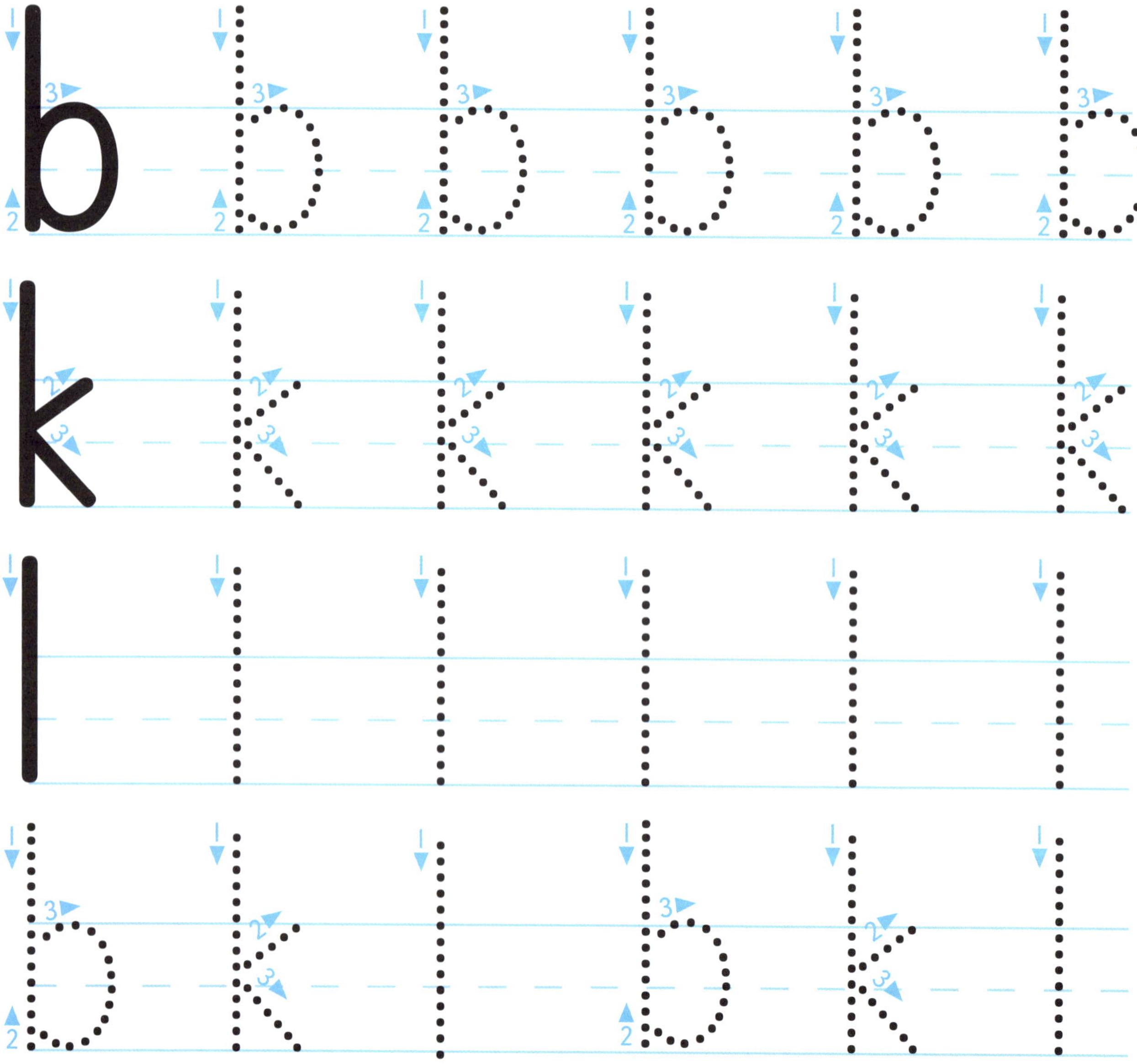

b b b b b b

k k k k k k

l l l l l l

b k b k

 Colour balloons with **d** in red and balloons with **b** in blue.

d   b

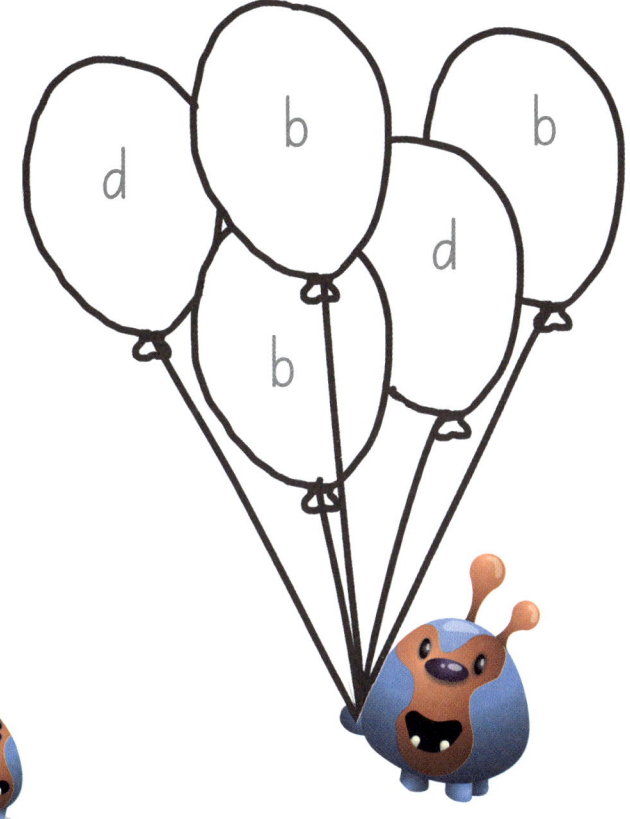

Can you make letters without writing them?

Play with writing.

Colour or paint a piece of paper in rainbow colours then cover in black crayon. Gently scratch out letters in the black to reveal colour.

Make letters with stones or shells.

Write the letters on a whiteboard or with chalk on a blackboard.

Give yourself a sticker

Now – track how you're doing on page 32!

Dots and lines (i, j and t)

 Trace these letters.

i j t

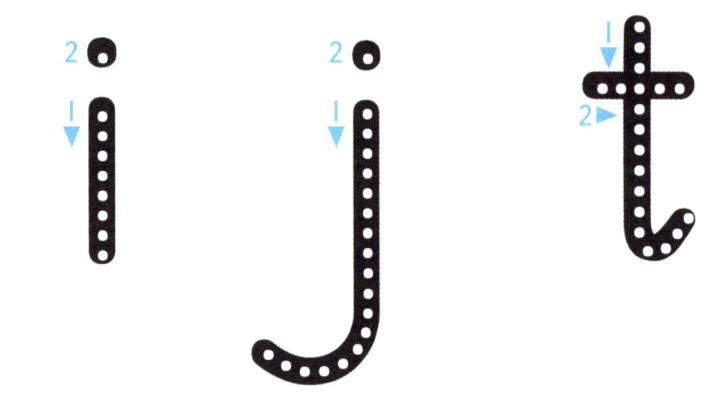

Look out! These letters are in two parts.

 Trace the letters.

i i i i i i

j j j j j j

t t t t t t

i j t i j t

 Match the objects to the letters.

i

j

t

Can you juggle with jelly whilst jumping in June?

Give yourself a sticker

Now – track how you're doing on page 32!

Up and under (u, y and p)

 Trace these letters.

To write **p**, start at the top, go down, then all the way back to the top and round.

Trace the letters.

Remember to make the top part of **y** and **p** sit on the line.

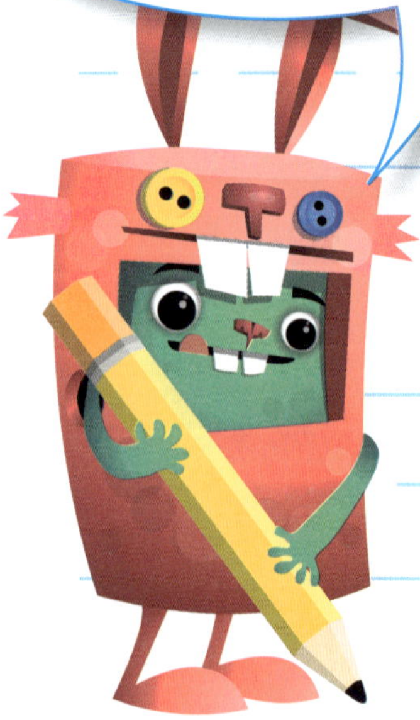

u

y

p

 Find the stickers of the fish to match the bowl.

m

y

p

u

q

g

 Play with writing.

Thread some pasta tubes on to string and make some letter shapes.

Be a letter detective – can you find letters **u**, **y** or **p** around your home?

Give yourself a sticker

Now – track how you're doing on page 32!

Zigzags (v and w)

Trace these letters.

V W

Wow!

Trace the letters.

V ⋁ ⋁ ⋁ ⋁ ⋁

W ⋁⋁ ⋁⋁ ⋁⋁ ⋁⋁ ⋁⋁

⋁ ⋁⋁ ⋁ ⋁⋁ ⋁ ⋁⋁

⋁ ⋁⋁ ⋁ ⋁⋁ ⋁ ⋁⋁

 Draw the way for Jot to find Dot in each maze.

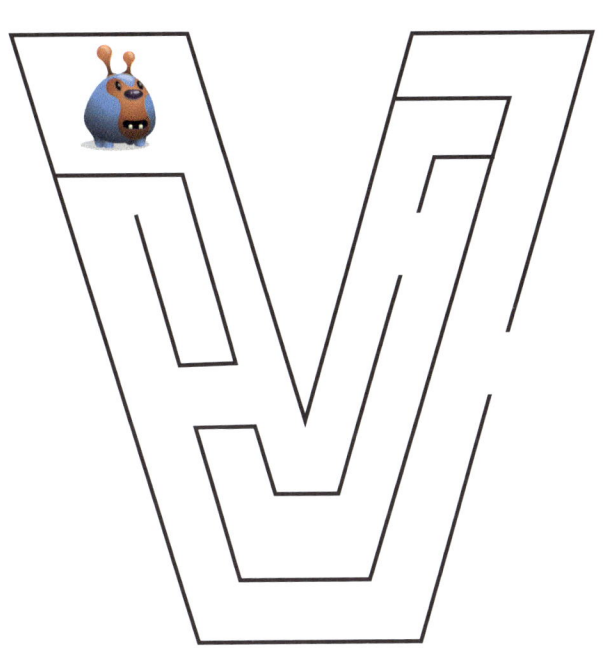

 You know nearly all the letters now!

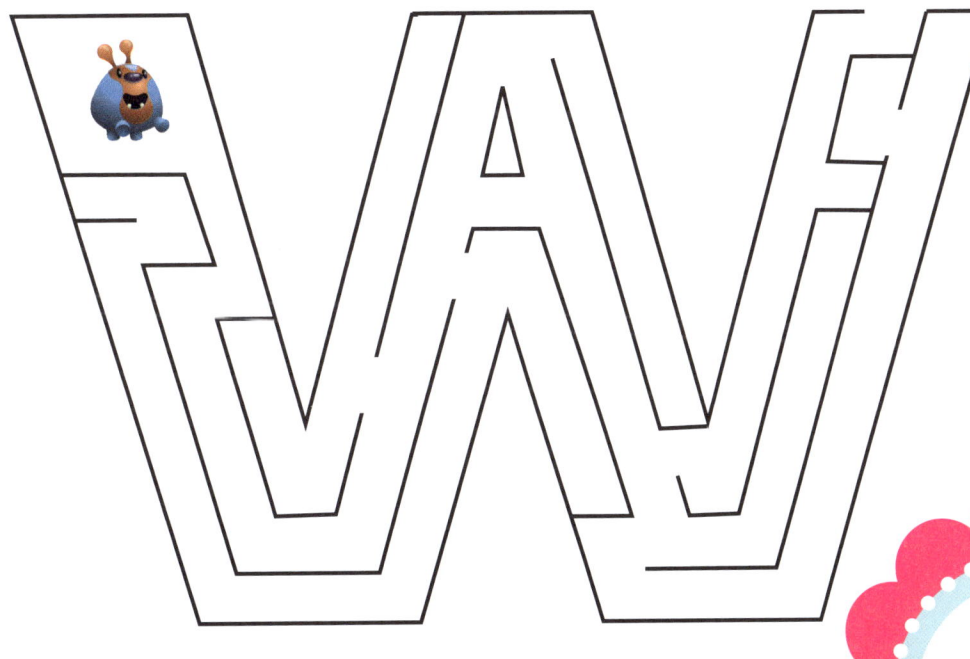

 Play with writing.

Write the letter **w** on an outside wall using water and a paintbrush.

Make the letters **v** and **w** using outdoor sticks or lollipop sticks.

Give yourself a sticker

Now – track how you're doing on page 32!

Crosses and zigzags (z and x)

 Trace these letters.

Z X

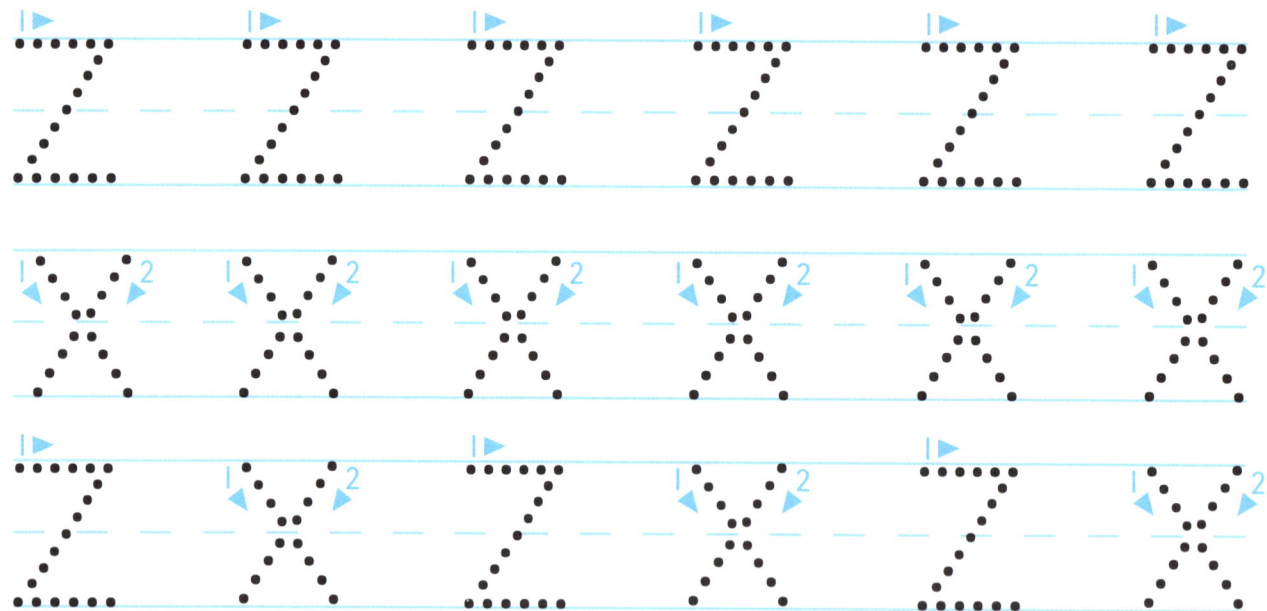

You need to write the letter 'x' in two parts.

 Trace the letters.

Z Z Z Z Z Z

X X X X X X

Z X Z X Z X

 Trace the words.

zoo   fix

 Draw zig-zag and dotty patterns on the snails.

I love snails.

Give yourself a sticker

Play with writing.

Can you chalk the letters **z** and **x** on the ground outdoors?

Make a map and include an **x** to mark the spot where the buried treasure is hidden.

Now – track how you're doing on page 32!

More words

Trace these words.

You can write!

mum   nap

dad   can

cog   and   but

was   fix

Give yourself a sticker

Write your name.

Now – track how you're doing on page 32!

The alphabet

✏️ Trace over the alphabet.

a b c d e

f g h i j k

l m n o p q

r s t u v w

x y z

Now – track how you're doing on page 32!

31

You did it! You wrote all the letters. Copy them again.

Have more fun writing letters.

Progress Chart

Colour in a face.

Page	I Can . . .	How did you do?
2–3	I can follow lines with my finger.	😊 😐 🙁
4–5	I can hold a pencil correctly.	😊 😐 🙁
6–7	I can make marks with my pencil.	😊 😐 🙁
8–9	I can trace lines with my pencil.	😊 😐 🙁
10–11	I can write the letters c, a and o.	😊 😐 🙁
12–13	I can write the letters d, g and q.	😊 😐 🙁
14–15	I can write the letters e, f and s.	😊 😐 🙁
16–17	I can write the letters r and m.	😊 😐 🙁
18	I can write the letters n and h.	😊 😐 🙁
19	I can write some words.	😊 😐 🙁
20–21	I can write the letters b, k and l.	😊 😐 🙁
22–23	I can write the letters i, j and t.	😊 😐 🙁
24–25	I can write the letters u, y and p.	😊 😐 🙁
26–27	I can write the letters v and w.	😊 😐 🙁
28–29	I can write x and z.	😊 😐 🙁
30–31	I can write more words and all the letters.	😊 😐 🙁

How did YOU do?